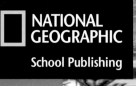

NATIONAL GEOGRAPHIC
School Publishing

Places on Earth

Annabelle Tan

PICTURE CREDITS

Cover, 4 (below left), 7, 9, 10, 11, 12, 14 (right), 16 (above left, below center), Photolibrary.com; 1 (above left & below right), 4 (above left), 5 (all), 13, 14 (above left), 15 (above), 16 (above center, below left & below right), APL/Corbis; 1 (above right), 15 (below), APL; 1 (below left), 8, 14 (below left), Getty Images; 2, 4 (right), 6, 16 (above right), Lonely Planet Images.

Produced through the worldwide resources of the National Geographic Society, John M. Fahey, Jr., President and Chief Executive Officer; Gilbert M. Grosvenor, Chairman of the Board; Nina D. Hoffman, Executive Vice President and President, Books and Education Publishing Group.

PREPARED BY NATIONAL GEOGRAPHIC SCHOOL PUBLISHING

Ericka Markman, Senior Vice President and President Children's Books and Education Publishing Group; Steve Mico, Senior Vice President and Publisher; Marianne Hiland, Editorial Director; Lynnette Brent, Executive Editor; Michael Murphy and Barbara Wood, Senior Editors; Bea Jackson, Design Director; David Dumo, Art Director; Margaret Sidlowsky, Illustrations Director; Matt Wascavage, Manager of Publishing Services; Sean Philpotts, Production Manager.

MANUFACTURING AND QUALITY MANAGEMENT

Christopher A. Liedel, Chief Financial Officer; Phillip L. Schlosser, Director; Clifton M. Brown III, Manager.

BOOK DEVELOPMENT

Ibis for Kids Australia Pty Limited.

Published by the National Geographic Society
1145 17th Street, N.W.
Washington, D.C. 20036-4688

ISBN 0-7922-6050-3

Fourth Printing 2008
Printed in China

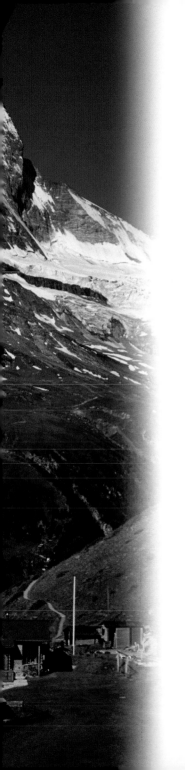

Contents

Think and Discuss

forest

desert

Look at all these places on Earth! What do you know about these places?

mountain

wetland

plain

Hot Places

Some places on Earth are hot.

This town is in a hot desert.

This house is in a hot rain forest.

Cold Places

Some places on Earth are cold.

This town is near cold mountains.

This fox is on a cold plain.

Dry Places

Some places on Earth are dry.

This city is on a dry plain.

This snake is in a dry desert.

Wet Places

Some places on Earth are wet.

This town is by a river.

This house is in a wetland.

Tell about the place where you live. How is it like these places?

desert

forest

mountain

place

plain

river

wetland

15

Picture Glossary

desert

forest

mountain

plain

river

wetland